Our World of Information

Look It Up

Finding Information

Claire Throp

Heinemann Library,
Chicago, IL

www.heinemannraintree.com
Visit our website to find out more information about Heinemann-Raintree books.

To order:
☎ Phone 888-454-2279
🖳 Visit www.heinemannraintree.com to browse our catalog and order online.

Edited by Rebecca Rissman and Catherine Veitch
Designed by Richard Parker
Original illustrations © Capstone Global Library
Illustrated by Darren Lingard
Picture research by Ruth Blair
Production by Duncan Gilbert
Originated by Heinemann Library
Printed in China by South China Printing Company Ltd.

14 13 12 11 10
10 9 8 7 6 5 4 3

Library of Congress Cataloging-in-Publication Data
Throp, Claire.
  Look it up : finding information / Claire Throp.
    p. cm. -- (Our world of information)
  Includes bibliographical references and index.
  ISBN 978-1-4329-3371-5 -- ISBN 978-1-4329-3377-7 (pbk.)
1. Information resources--Juvenile literature. 2. Information retrieval--Juvenile literature. I. Title.
  ZA3070.T48 2009
  020--dc22
                    2009004405

Acknowledgements

We would like to thank the following for permission to reproduce photographs: Alamy pp. **6** (© StockShot), **11** (© Mitch Diamond), **19** (© Ian Shaw), **17** (© Jupiterimages/ Polka Dot), **21** (© Greatstock Photographic Library), **27** (© Richard G. Bingham II); © Capstone Publishers pp. **8** & **26** (Karon Dubke); Corbis p. **10** (Michael Keller); Getty Images p. **5** (Tim Platt); Photoshot p. **24** (Asiaimages); Shutterstock p. **12** (© kwest).

Cover photograph of a girl reaching for a book reproduced with permission of Corbis (Tim Pannell).

Every effort has been made to contact copyright holders of any material reproduced in this book. Any omissions will be rectified in subsequent printings if notice is given to the publisher.

All the Internet addresses (URLs) given in this book were valid at the time of going to press. However, due to the dynamic nature of the Internet, some addresses may have changed, or sites may have changed or ceased to exist since publication. While the author and publisher regret any inconvenience this may cause readers, no responsibility for any such changes can be accepted by either the author or the publisher.

Contents

Any words appearing in the text in bold, **like this**, are explained in the glossary.

Information In Our World

 How many different **sources** of information can you see here?

You are surrounded by information. Information is what people know about things. It includes photographs, signs, **symbols**, sounds, and words that tell you how to do things or where to go.

In your everyday life you often need to find certain types of information. You might need information for a school project or about a new hobby. This book will help you find what you need.

At school, you sometimes need to work on projects in a group.

Questions

One of the quickest ways to find information is to ask questions. First, decide who will know the answer. Then, think about how to word your question. Sometimes you will need to ask or answer more questions after you get an answer.

 Make sure that you stay safe. Only ask a stranger for help if you are with an adult.

Be polite and listen carefully when you ask for information. The person you ask may suggest that you talk to another person or look at printed information.

 Can you think of a clearer question for this boy to ask?

Printed Information

Libraries are great places to find all kinds of information.

Printed information comes in many forms, including books and newspapers. There are two types of books: fiction and **nonfiction**. Story books are fiction. Nonfiction books, such as encyclopedias and dictionaries, give you facts rather than stories.

In a library, ask a librarian or use a catalog to find the information you are looking for. A librarian can help you find a book by using the **Dewey Decimal System**. You can also use an **online catalog** that lists information **sources** found in the library.

To find a book in a library, you need to follow a special system. A librarian can help you to understand this system.

Useful Features

 Use the features in a book to help you find the information you want.

Once you have found the book that you want, there are **features** inside it that will help you to find the exact information you need. A table of contents lists the headings for each part of the book. Look at the table of contents in this book for an example.

An index is an alphabetical list of subjects found within the book. Entries in encyclopedias and dictionaries are usually alphabetical, too.

 It is much easier to look for a particular topic when the entries are arranged in alphabetical order.

Organizing Information

Funnel-web spider ← main heading

Funnel-webs are large spiders. They are found in eastern Australia and Tasmania, in forests along the coast.

Spider burrows ← subheading

Funnel-web spiders live in burrows under rocks and rotting logs. The burrows have funnel-shaped entrances and are lined with silky webs. Males leave their burrows in summer to find females to mate with. At this time, they sometimes wander into people's homes, yards, and swimming pools.

The funnel-web is one of the world's deadliest spiders. If a person is bitten, they need to get medical help fast. ← caption

The main heading on a page tells you what kind of information is on that page. Smaller words are used in **subheadings**. Subheadings tell you what type of information is in the next paragraph. Captions describe what appears in a photograph or artwork. They usually give more information.

Nonfiction books often have a **glossary**. This is an alphabetical list of words that may be difficult to understand or need further explanation. Words in the book that can be found in the glossary are usually shown in bold lettering.

Glossary

database way of storing and organizing information

features characteristics or appearance of an object

graphic organizer way of showing information in a chart, table, or graph

keyword word that describes the particular subject you want to find information about

menu offers a list of subjects included as web pages on a website. The menu of a website is like a table of contents. If you choose one of the things on the list, you can jump to that subject.

nonfiction text that is factual rather than made up like in a story

online connected to the Internet

online catalog electronic list of all the information sources, such as books, movies, and magazines, that can be found in a particular library. The list can be accessed by computer.

podcast recorded program of talk or music that can be taken off the Internet and listened to at any time

reliable trustworthy

search engine website that provides lists of other websites about a particular subject

source place in which we can find things such as information. Books, magazines, and the Internet are all sources of information.

symbol word or picture that stands for something else. For example, a triangle made up of three arrows is the sign for recycling.

web name given to the interconnected websites on the Internet. The web is similar to a spider web. Like a spider web, the websites are connected.

web browser program on your computer that allows you to view websites

web page term used to describe one page of a website. A website is often made up of many web pages. The main or starting page of a website is called the home page.

wiki website that allows many people to add or change information

30

Graphic Organizers

Information does not just have to appear as words and pictures. **Graphic organizers** can also be very helpful. Sometimes looking at information in a graph, table, or chart makes it much easier to understand.

 This is called a line graph. It shows how things change over time.

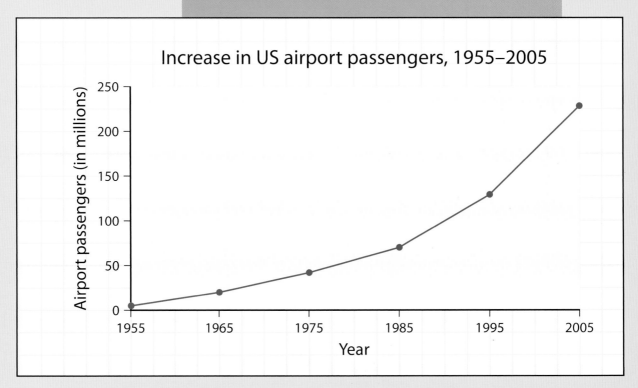

Number of children in Banbury School who own pets

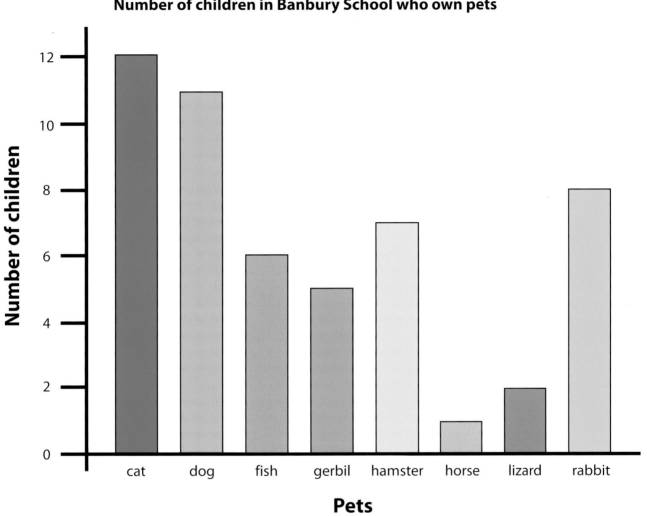

 This is called a bar graph. It shows how much of something there is.

Electronic Information

Electronic information includes **databases**, **online** encyclopedias and dictionaries, DVDs, Websites, **wikis**, and **podcasts**.

TIC Travel Information Center

Home | Search | Our Collection | Thesaurus | About Us | My TIC

Search TIC Collection

Search Term(s):

Search in:

» Advanced Search
» Thesaurus
» Help

Search

Records added in the last month: **3278**

A database is a collection of information stored electronically. To find information in a database you need to search using **keywords**.

Podcasts can be listened to at any time on a computer or an MP3 player. They cover a wide range of topics. You can either sign up to receive new episodes as soon as they are available or click on them one by one.

 You can listen to a podcast or view a video online.

The Internet

The Internet links together computers all over the world. This means people can view information stored or created on other computers. Information on the Internet includes Websites, encyclopedias, newspapers, Email, **wikis**, and social networks. You can use Email to contact people anywhere.

Most information on the Internet can be found on Websites. Websites can be set up by governments, organizations, or ordinary people.

Not all information on the Internet is good or **reliable**. You should check with an adult before using a Website you find.

Searching the Internet

The best way to look up information online is to use a **search engine**. A search engine looks through all the Websites on the Internet to find the ones that might be helpful.

You should use **keywords** when you search the Internet. These are words that describe the subject you want to find out about.

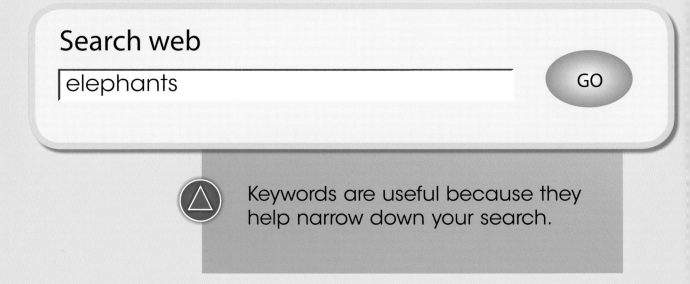

Search web

elephants | GO

⚠ Keywords are useful because they help narrow down your search.

If you type in several keywords rather than just one, the search engine provides a much shorter list of Websites.

Websites

There are millions of Websites on the Internet. Websites usually have a number of separate pages within them. These pages, called **web pages**, can include text, pictures, sound, and video.

 Some Websites are created just for children. Others may have a special section for children.

You can go to different parts of a Website by clicking on the **menu**. This is found on the home page, which is usually the opening page of a Website. Sometimes the menu is found on every page of a Website.

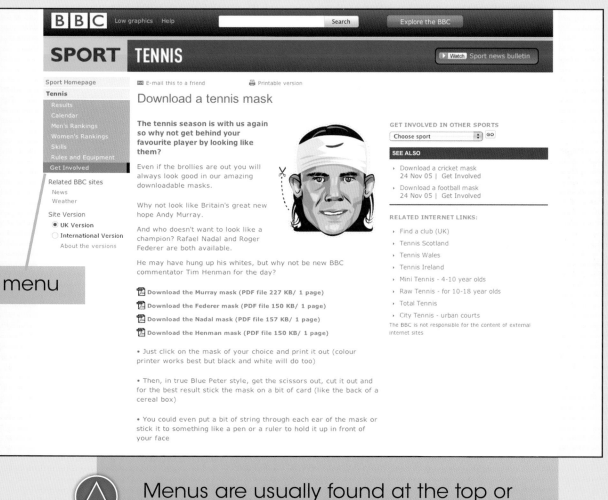

menu

Menus are usually found at the top or on the left-hand side of a web page.

Beware!

 If a Website looks strange to you, or if you cannot find out who the author or creator of the **web page** is, ask an adult for help.

Not all Websites contain **reliable** information. Remember, anyone can put together a Website. It is a good idea to look at the Websites of well-known organizations such as museums and government Websites such as NASA.

When you look at a Website, you have to be careful about where you click. Some Websites include advertisements, which try to sell things to people who use the Website. Be careful about the information you find on Websites that have advertisements.

What Comes Next?

There is a lot of information available. It can sometimes be difficult to find what you want. Asking questions, looking at books, and searching the Internet are just some of the ways you can find new information.

 Stay on top of all the information you find by being organized.

Sometimes it helps to talk things through with a friend.

Once you have looked at many different **sources** of information, you then need to sort it out. You need to choose which information is the most useful and **reliable** for what you want to do.

Activities

Practice Makes Perfect

Practice what you have learned in this book. Search for information about a musical instrument on the Internet by using keywords. Before you begin, think about the question you want to answer.

- Do you want to know the different types of instrument?

- Do you want to know about one type of instrument?

Use keywords that will best help you find the information you seek. Gradually change or add to the keywords to narrow down your search.

Always ask for help if you need it.

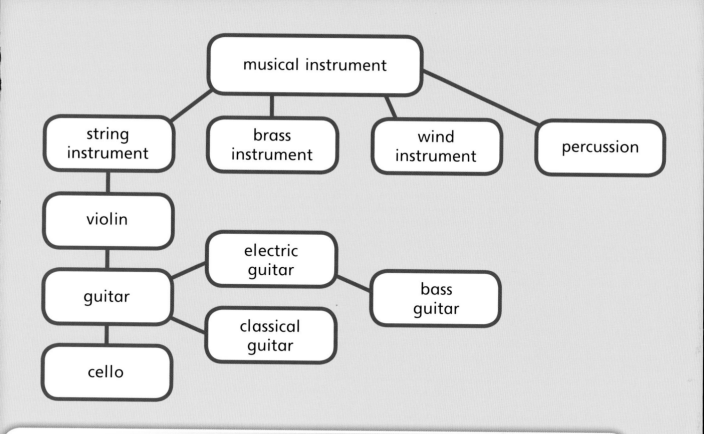

Fake Websites—How Good Are Your Detective Skills?

You should not believe everything you see or read on the Internet. Make a list of things that tell you that these are fake or bogus Websites:

- Does the Jackalope exist? (Look at the Website www.sudftw.com/jackcon)
- Do you believe that dog island is a real place? (www.thedogisland.com/)
- Do you believe there really is a tree octopus? (http://zapatopi.net/treeoctopus/)

Glossary

database way of storing and organizing information

Dewey Decimal System number system that libraries use to organize books on the shelves

features characteristics or appearance of an object

glossary alphabetical list of words that may be difficult to understand

graphic organizer way of showing information in a chart, table, or graph

keyword word that describes the particular subject you want to find information about

menu list of subjects included as web pages on a Website. The menu of a Website is like a table of contents. If you choose one of the things on the list, you can jump to that subject.

nonfiction book that is factual rather than made up

online connected to the Internet

online catalog electronic list of all the information sources, such as books, movies, and magazines, that can be found in a particular library. The list can be accessed by computer.

podcast recorded program of spoken words or music that can be taken off the Internet and listened to anytime

reliable trustworthy

search engine Website that provides lists of other Websites about a particular subject

source place where you can find information. Books, magazines, and the Internet are all sources of information.

subheading paragraph heading

symbol word or picture that stands for something else. For example, a triangle made up of three arrows is the sign for recycling.

web page term used to describe one page of a Website. A Website is often made up of many web pages. The main or starting page of a Website is called the home page.

wiki Website that allows many people to add or change information

Find Out More

Books

Oxlade, Chris. *My First Email Guide.* Chicago, Ill.: Heinemann Library, 2007.

Oxlade, Chris. *My First Internet Guide.* Chicago, Ill.: Heinemann Library, 2007.

Websites

KidsClick! Worlds of Web Searching
www.kidsclick.org/wows/
Learn valuable lessons in how to search the World Wide Web.

IPL Kidspace
www.ipl.org/div/kidspace/
This Website is like a public library online.

CBBC – Stay Safe
www.bbc.co.uk/cbbc/help/safesurfing
This Website gives you advice on staying safe while you are on the Internet.

Homework Help – Yahoo! Kids
http://kids.yahoo.com/learn
This web page includes links to an encyclopedia, dictionary, maps, and a lot of other useful Websites.

Ask Kids – Schoolhouse
www.askkids.com/schoolhouse?pch=sch
Ask Kids is a search engine created just for kids.

Index